Ancient Roman CULTURE

Amelie von Zumbusch

Published in 2014 by The Rosen Publishing Group, Inc.
29 East 21st Street, New York, NY 10010

First Edition

Book Design: Kate Vlachos
Layout Design: Andrew Povolny

Library of Congress Cataloging-in-Publication Data

Zumbusch, Amelie von.
  Ancient Roman culture / by Amelie von Zumbusch. — First edition.
      pages cm. — (Spotlight on ancient civilizations: Rome)
  Includes index.
  ISBN 978-1-4777-0775-3 (library binding) — ISBN 978-1-4777-0883-5 (pbk.) — ISBN 978-1-4777-0884-2 (6-pack)
  1. Rome—Civilization—Juvenile literature. I. Title.
  DG77.Z86 2014
  937—dc23
                                          2012045398

Manufactured in the United States of America

CPSIA Compliance Information: Batch #S13PK2: For Further Information contact Rosen Publishing, New York, New York at 1-800-237-9932

CONTENTS

Drawing from Other Cultures

Have you ever read a book or seen a movie that was set in ancient Rome? Historians believe that Roman **civilization** started in the eighth century BC and lasted until the fifth century AD. The civilization was centered around the city of Rome, in what is now Italy.

This carving is from a Roman sarcophagus, or stone coffin. It shows a scene from the life of the Greek hero Achilles.

Roman culture spread to lands that the Romans conquered. The Romans built these columns in Apamea, in what is now Syria.

Ancient Rome had a rich culture. Culture is the beliefs, practices, and arts of a group of people. Roman culture borrowed from nearby cultures, including the cultures of people that the Romans **conquered**, or defeated. The Greeks had a huge influence on Roman culture. The Etruscans, who lived northeast of Rome, were another influence.

The Roman Pantheon

The Romans worshiped a **pantheon**, or group of gods. They believed that different gods had power over different areas. Jupiter was the ruler of the gods and the god of the sky. His wife, Juno, protected Rome and was associated with women and marriage. Mars was the god of war, while Venus was the goddess of love. Minerva was the goddess of crafts and wisdom. She later became associated with war, too.

Many Roman gods match up with gods in the Greek pantheon. Jupiter is like the Greek god Zeus, while Juno resembles the Greek goddess Hera.

The emperor Hadrian had the Pantheon built in about AD 126. The temple honored all of Rome's gods. It replaced an earlier Pantheon that had been built by Marcus Agrippa.

Religion in Roman Homes

Alongside the Roman pantheon, some Romans worshiped gods or goddesses from other cultures. The Egyptian goddess Isis was popular. So was Cybele, a goddess from what is now Turkey.

The Mithraic mysteries were one of several religions that spread to Rome. They were popular in the Roman military and focused on Mithras, seen in this Roman sculpture.

This lararium painting comes from the Roman city of Pompeii. It is one of many paintings that were preserved when Pompeii was buried after a volcano erupted in AD 79.

The Romans also worshiped spirits, such as the *Penates*. These household spirits were associated with storerooms. The *genius* was the spirit of the head of a family. Spirits known as *Lares* were also important.

Every Roman house had a shrine called a *lararium*, where the members of the household made offerings to Lares and other spirits. These offerings were often foods, such as milk, fruit, or wine.

Religion and the Roman State

Romans worshiped the goddess of the hearth, Vesta, in their homes. A hearth is a fireplace. Vesta was also worshiped in a big temple in Rome's forum, or public center. Women called Vestal Virgins served in this temple. They were among the most powerful women in Rome.

You can see the ruins, or remains, of the Temple of Vesta in the Roman Forum to this day.

The Roman Forum had many temples. The Roman government supported these temples. In them, priests made official offerings to the gods. Other priests tried to figure out messages from the gods. In later years, Roman **emperors,** or rulers, were often declared gods after they died. The Romans built temples honoring them, too.

Rome's first emperor, Augustus, died on August 19, in the year AD 14. He was deified, or declared to be a god, that September.

Spectator Sports

Sports played an important role in Roman culture. The Romans loved **chariot** races. The Circus Maximus was the main **stadium** used for races. It held more than 100,000 **spectators**, or watchers.

Roman charioteers, or chariot racers, belonged to either the red, white, blue, or green team. Here a member of the white team holds one of his horses.

Gladiatorial games were held in the Colosseum after that huge building was finished in AD 80. You can visit its ruins in Rome.

Events at which **gladiators** fought to the death, called gladiatorial games, were also very popular. These were originally held in honor of people who had died. Later, the Roman government started backing gladiatorial fights. Most gladiators fought against other gladiators, but some fought against animals.

Romans generally preferred watching sports to taking part in them. Gladiators and chariot drivers were usually prisoners of war, **slaves,** or former slaves.

Roman Philosophy

Philosophy is the study of the basic nature of things. Several Greek schools of philosophy became popular among the Romans. Epicureanism was started by the Greek philosopher Epicurus of Samos. He believed that the point of life is to gain pleasure by avoiding pain. The Roman poet Lucretius was an Epicurean.

Marcus Aurelius wrote a book called *Meditations* that explained his ideas about Stoicism.

You can see the ruins of the Pecile at the emperor Hadrian's home in Tivoli, Italy. It was modeled on the Stoa Poikile, where Zeno, the founder of Stoicism, had taught in Athens, Greece.

Stoicism was very popular in Rome. Stoics believed that everything in the universe was ordered by natural law and that people should live by the laws of nature. They thought people should accept the world around them and avoid extremes. The Roman emperor Marcus Aurelius was a leading Stoic.

Painting and Sculpture

The Romans borrowed many artistic styles from the Greeks. However, Roman portraits tended to be more realistic. Portraits are pictures or sculptures of real people. They were important in Roman culture. Some Romans believed that having portraits of people who had died would keep their ghosts from haunting you!

Wall paintings were common in Roman homes. These were often landscapes or scenes with people. Roman artists also made paintings on moveable boards.

Many Roman sculptures honored public leaders or celebrated war victories. Tombs were often decorated with sculptures, too. Wax portrait masks, called *imagines,* were used in funeral **processions**.

This fresco shows a funeral procession. Frescoes are paintings that are done on freshly laid plaster. Roman wall paintings were often frescoes.

ΛΛΧΙΩΝ

ANTIΓONA

17

Lasting Architecture

Architecture is the art of designing buildings. The Romans developed many new architectural ideas. They invented a better kind of concrete and became the first people to use concrete widely. They also found new ways to use arches in their buildings. They built long **aqueducts** to carry fresh water to Roman towns. These were designed at the perfect angle so that the water could always flow slightly downhill.

The Romans built aqueducts throughout they lands they ruled. For example, they built this one in what is now Tarragona, Spain.

This mosaic of the Greek hero Alexander the Great was found in the House of the Faun, in the buried Roman city of Pompeii.

You can still see the ruins, or remains, of many Roman buildings today. Some of these are decorated with **mosaics**, or pictures made of many tiny pieces of tile or stone.

Latin Literature

The Romans spoke a language called Latin. To this day, people learn Latin so that they can read the great works that were written in it. Historians, such as Tacitus and Suetonius, explored Rome's history. Cicero wrote about philosophy and politics. Pliny the Elder wrote on science.

Cicero was a statesman and lawyer as well as a writer. His full name was Marcus Tullius Cicero.

This wall painting shows Aeneas and his son Ascanius during their long flight from their home city of Troy.

Rome produced many great poets, such as Ovid, Juvenal, and Horace. The best-known is probably Virgil. He wrote a long poem called the *Aeneid*. It tells the story of Aeneas, who flees to Italy after his home in what is now Turkey was destroyed. Members of his family are said to have founded Rome.

Rome's Lasting Influence

Roman plays drew heavily on Greek plays. Funny plays, called comedies, were most popular. Terence and Plautus were well-known Roman comedy writers. Seneca wrote tragedies, which tell stories that end badly. Actors in plays were always men. Plays were originally performed during festivals. Festivals included many entertainments, such as acrobats, jugglers, mimes, and reenactments of sea battles.

Some of the theaters in which plays were performed still stand. Roman culture continues to be a powerful force, too. It has inspired people for thousands of years.

Ancient Rome still fascinates people. Here, tourists visit Pompeii, the Roman city that was buried by volcanic ash. The ash helped preserve much of Pompeii.

GLOSSARY

aqueducts (A-kweh-dukts) Channels or pipes used to carry water for long distances.

chariot (CHAR-ee-ut) A two-wheeled battle car pulled by horses.

civilization (sih-vih-lih-ZAY-shun) People living in a certain way.

conquered (KON-kerd) Overcame.

emperors (EM-per-erz) Rulers of empires or of several countries.

gladiators (GLA-dee-ay-turz) People who fought to the death against other people or animals.

mosaics (moh-ZAY-iks) Pictures made by fitting together small pieces of stone, glass, or tile and pasting them in place.

pantheon (PAN-thee-on) The group of gods that a people worship.

processions (pruh-SESH-unz) Groups of people moving along in an orderly way for a special purpose or occasion.

slaves (SLAYVZ) People who are "owned" by other people and forced to work for them.

spectators (SPEK-tay-terz) People who see or watch something without taking an active part.

stadium (STAY-dee-um) A place where sports are played.

INDEX

WEBSITES

Due to the changing nature of Internet links, PowerKids Press has developed an online list of websites related to the subject of this book. This site is updated regularly. Please use this link to access the list:
www.powerkidslinks.com/sacr/cult/